Weathering The Digital Storm

How To Fortify Your Digital Growth Strategies In Unpredictable Times

Lisa Apolinski

INDIE BOOKS
INTERNATIONAL

ISBN-10: 1-947480-59-6
ISBN-13: 978-1-947480-59-9
Library of Congress Control Number:2019907305

Designed by Joni McPherson, mcphersongraphics.com

INDIE BOOKS INTERNATIONAL, LLC
2424 VISTA WAY, SUITE 316
OCEANSIDE, CA 92054

www.indiebooksintl.com

Contents

TABLE OF CONTENTS

Preface

The more I delve into and work with the world of digital engagement, the more I am humbled by it. This is primarily because of the overwhelming power digital engagement has to impact our organizations and the consumers of our products and services.

My purpose for writing this book is a bold one: I want to prepare you and your organizations for the potentially perilous and ever-changing road ahead in the digital revolution. Digital growth strategies will need to be reimagined constantly to continue to be effective—in essence, digital growth is like scaling a mountain with no peak. But this climb, while continuous and difficult at times, can bring insight, growth, and strength to your organization. The most important takeaway is you are never finished with your digital strategy—there is always work to be done and new discoveries to be made.

Lisa Apolinski
Phoenix, AZ
February 2019

Chapter 1

Why You Need A Fortified Digital Growth Strategy

Surprising statistic: Studies have shown that over 85 percent of customer engagement will happen online during the course of a conversion cycle. That number soon could be as high as 90 percent, and will no doubt continue to rise.

In this day and age, consumers can use a mobile device to purchase food, supplies, travel, even a new car. Even tax preparation is digital; chat with a certified accountant can be accomplished online.

Let's turn that statistic on its head. Ten percent of your conversations and engagements with customers will happen via phone, mail, or in person (twenty years ago, those were the *only* engagement channels available for use with your customer pool). That makes digital marketing the single most important aspect of communication with prospects as they move through a conversion cycle.

Think about early technological advancements such as the telephone or the automobile. With those advancements came long periods for the general population to adopt and adapt. With current technology (and subsequently, digital engagement), that window is now measured in months versus years. The adoption window will continue to shorten as new advancements emerge. In order for organizations to stay on top, they almost have to anticipate new trends applicable to their audiences. And since these changes come quickly, there will always be a list of new digital tasks to do and knowledge to gain.

If we return to our customer statistic (85 percent will communicate with you via digital methods) and evidence that indicates that percentage will likely rise in the next few years, fortifying your digital strategy is a critical piece of being able to continue to reach your customer. You certainly would not let your phone lines go down or lock your doors so customers could not come in to buy your products. Would you be OK with a phone connection full of static or physical barriers around your store that customers had to navigate? I would venture to say those would also result in a resounding *no*. If those barriers are not acceptable, then why do organizations tolerate a website where information is difficult to find or emails that feel like the digital version of robocalls? These subpar user experiences not only turn off customers to your brand, but also open the door for market share erosion.

Some critics and even experts say digital engagement is simpler than people have been led to believe; they suggest that as long as you have a website and send out a few emails, you have done your digital duty. Some critics will tell you that digital engagement is just too complex, so there is no way to optimize. And some say that because digital technology changes so frequently, there is no point in trying to optimize. While these considerations may be easy to accept because then there is no responsibility (digital things *simply happen* to our organizations), this is a gross miscalculation.

Certainly, organizations would either like to throw their hands up and say it is just too complex, or cheer for themselves because they have taken care of their digital marketing and they can now move on to other things. From working with organizations around the world, I have discovered these notions are based more on lack of understanding of our own power to engage in the digital space than on anything else. Knowing is half the battle, and by knowing where you have digital holes (in both your strategy and knowledge), you can educate and apply yourself to closing those gaps, or at the very least, work with the right experts who can guide you to a better digital future for your organization and your customers. Organizations can look at both sides of this argument and see how different points of view result in very different business outcomes.

Ready To Talk Lingerie

Consider a company that has clearly done its digital homework and has even been called a "tech-minded organization" by Bloomberg.[1] Founded in 2013, ThirdLove launched by using mobile video ads delivered through Facebook. In fact, Facebook uses ThirdLove results in a case study on best practices for mobile video ads. ThirdLove only sells products online, has grown over the past five years, and was added to *Business Insider's* list of lingerie companies that are changing the industry in July 2018.[2] The company's use of digital engagement, including its trademarked FitFinder quiz and use of digital advertising, allowed ThirdLove to reduce the cost of user acquisition and cost per click (CPC) by 25 percent. What's more, when customers purchase from the company, they can take the quiz, order their product, try it at home for a period of time, and return it if it isn't *exactly* what they want without ever having to venture out of the digital retail space. Facebook was even quick to share the backstory of ThirdLove and the moment the cofounder

[1] "Tech Is at the Heart of ThirdLove's Success, Co-CEO Heidi Zak Says." Bloomberg.com. October 05, 2018. Accessed February 21, 2019. https://www.bloomberg.com/news/videos/2018-10-05/tech-is-at-the-heart-of-thirdlove-s-success-co-ceo-heidi-zak-says-video.

[2] Leighton, Mara. "6 New Lingerie Companies That Are Changing the Industry - with Inclusive Sizes and a Woman-led Design Process." Business Insider. July 08, 2018. Accessed February 21, 2019. https://www.businessinsider.com/new-lingerie-brands-2018-6.

decided to launch a lingerie brand because none of the bras in her dresser drawer fit properly: Google "Why was ThirdLove created?" for a fascinating sidenote.

Compare that with an established brand, Victoria's Secret, which has seen a decline in sales over the last few years, with a significant drop in sales in 2018. Interestingly, when surveyed, more than half the brand's shoppers felt the brand had a "forced" or "fake" feeling.[3] Reviewing Victoria's Secret and the brand's digital presence, you can certainly check off boxes: website, emails, social media presence. But potential customers saying the brand is *forced* is telling—there is not a cohesive and appropriate brand message aligned with the current consumer climate. And this digital story misstep is costing the brand market share to new companies that, while barely old enough to walk, are running over an established brand.

This does not mean that Victoria's Secret is *bad* and ThirdLove is *good*. Clearly, Victoria's Secret has done amazing brand work in the past and is still a well-known brand name. This also does not mean that Victoria's Secret is on the verge of Game Over, as some business experts may be suggesting. What this does indicate, however, is that Victoria's Secret has clearly lost some conversion momentum due to a lack of consistent,

---

[3] Clipped wings: Victoria's Secret sales slip as shoppers become less daring." TheGuardian.com. July 22, 2018. Accessed February 21, 2019. https://www.theguardian.com/business/2018/jul/22/victorias-secret-pink-sales-stock-down.

measured focus on digital engagement, digital consumer behavior, and drivers for purchasing lingerie. Furthermore, this suggests that a realignment of digital strategy and a rebirth of its digital brand story are still well within reach and can help move the company in the right direction. But in having to refocus and regain lost momentum, Victoria's Secret faces a game of catch-up. It appears that the company thought it had crossed the finish line in its digital communication when the race had not even started.

A Climb With No Summit

There are several lessons in this book and many insights into the digital space. Digital marketing is like a climb with no summit. Put another way, there is no finish line, so the race is never-ending. The only way to lose in this digital race is to not run. That is one thing I love about digital engagement. Anyone can gain strides in digital engagement at any time. Today, one company may be at the head of the pack, or maybe just starting the race, or maybe it has tripped and is just getting back up. Each day is a new opportunity to learn and try something new. The new digital strategy may fail miserably, and that is *great* because that offers another chance at digital learning and another opportunity to provide the best digital experience to clients.

If each day is another opportunity, it also means that each day creates a level playing field and can be used to anyone's advantage at any time. We are constantly evolving our brand and message, tweaking and adding to our digital channels and testing new technology for digital engagement.

When Victoria's Secret was at its height in the early 2000s, and digital engagement was not only brand new but still a new concept to most of the business world, a company like ThirdLove may not have found the space to launch or grow. At the very least, it would have been incredibly difficult to take market share from an established brand. But in this digital age, there is space for many different companies to share their brand stories and provide an amazing user experience. This is an environment where a strong competitive spirit and desire to learn are key factors in growing organizations.

Digital Engagement Is A Process, Not A Single Event

Creating access to billions of people around the globe twenty-four hours a day, digital engagement is not something an organization can set up and forget. Companies can learn, use, and test digital engagement over and over again. Any day a company wants to have a sale is a day in the digital engagement calendar. If a customer is not taking a day off from the company's digital house, neither should that company.

The digital world is not just complex or just simple—it is a little bit of both. The digital world is powerful and at the same time reachable. Digital technology provides unprecedented access to prospects while continuing to evolve in how well a connection is developed. Subsequent digital communication allows slow, sustained engagement within quick tests and fast digital fails. The juxtaposition of these attributes makes the digital world worthy of the challenge and exciting to enter. Just be ready for a long visit.

Consider an analogy: Most car accidents occur within twenty-five miles of the home. Driving in familiar surroundings or surroundings that a person encounters every day can cause drivers to relax, get comfortable, and lose their defensive driving edge. The driver is not daydreaming—accidents come from unanticipated and unpredictable events, such as another driver making a critical mistake or an animal running into the road. Likewise, unanticipated or unpredictable events are a part of life and certainly a part of an organization's environment. With economic turbulence, global trade wars, new competitors and other outside factors, there is almost always some kind of storm of events on the horizon, waiting to happen. But that also means there are potential opportunities to offer an outstanding user experience, strong digital engagement, and an authentic brand story. Companies can start paying attention when they perceive the home stretch.

With 85 percent of all customer engagement occurring in the digital space, the payoff for the hard work necessary to stay in that space is well worth the effort. An organization cannot afford to miss out on these engagement opportunities. There is always another competitor who can take advantage of the current business climate to throw digital strategy off. But before an organization invites prospects into their digital house, or takes on competitors in their space from a digital perspective, the digital house needs to be put in order.

Chapter 2

Modify Your Digital Message Now

The following is based on a true story; this organization's leaders were looking to change their digital message, but were not quite sure the best way to approach such an important task. All names and certain details have been changed in all stories in this book to maintain client confidentiality.

Bob's Dilemma

This is a story about Bob and his need for digital strategy support and assistance to properly modify his organization's digital message.

Bob was the director of marketing at a medical device organization. Despite his calm demeanor and knowledge of marketing, he had a huge task ahead of him. The founder, due to health concerns, had handed over day-to-day operations to his son. The son wanted to revitalize the company's brand, and with that, completely revamp the organization's digital presence. Bob was responsible for the task of maintaining the founder's vision while fulfilling this new brand direction.

He was also feeling frustrated—the company's brand was not effective in the digital space, and he needed help to change the digital engagement and make the brand more digitally relatable. He wanted to be sure he was approaching this initiative with the right strategy, keeping in consideration all of the current digital engagement best practices.

Bob brought me in to help him reinvent the company's digital message and brand without losing the essence of what made the brand's origin unique. He defined his finish line as setting a sales record for the following year after the new digital brand launch.

One of the main obstacles was that the original visual brand had been developed by the founder decades before, and that brand had been developed well before digital marketing went mainstream. Because of this, the original brand did not transfer well into the digital space. The organization had also matured in the industry and messaging needed to be updated to align with this growth and maturity.

When I shared this obstacle and its implications for digital engagement with Bob, he initially resisted. He said that, while he appreciated my advice, he would simply work with a freelancer to update the logo and add in the new brand colors. When Bob used an online service to do just that, he discovered the challenge of taking the original brand personality and translating it to the digital environment. What he received in new designs both missed the original brand story *and* failed to reflect the company's current energy and focus.

The new brand needed to not only reflect the current brand personality and work in both digital spaces and in print; this refreshed brand also needed to pay tribute and provide a respectful homage to the original brand feel. By providing a strong digital focus, including a color refresh and logo reimagining, the brand would have a modern feel and be digitally compatible.

The hard work was about to begin. As we brainstormed the core values of the organization, identified how customers and prospects should engage with the brand, and envisioned what words naturally connected with the organization, both Bob and the executive team embraced the mission. There were a few heated debates among members of the executive team, and the group discovered a brand personality and digital story that resonated and captured the essence of the company.

Digital Debut

When the new brand was launched at the main medical device industry trade show six months later, both customers and prospects offered positive feedback on the brand refresh, and the new brand was well received in the industry. The most interesting part of the brand refresh was that the colors were chosen to show vibrancy and engagement, and were very different from those of other major competitors. This color variation allowed the brand to stand out, both in print and in digital formats.

The president of the organization was impressed with Bob and the amazing year they had after the brand launch, due in part to the digital marketing work. The company's brand had gained heightened awareness, which resulted in strong gains in sales. As a result of the strong sales and positive brand recognition, Bob was given new business opportunities within the company.

This organization recognized that the brand and message that had worked in a pre-digital environment needed to be brought into the digital space. The organization had also matured, with new initiatives to impact the community and the industry. These new brand messages were vital to set the organization apart from others in the space.

As companies grow and mature, they will inevitably experience a digital evolution of their brand and messaging. This evolution should be seen as a natural progression and anticipated as an organization develops. Whether a company is young or a mature entity, the digital message and engagement should never go unreviewed.

Evolution And Revolution In The Digital Space

The volatile world of business has a nebulous quality that can quickly take over—and take down organizations. The Small Business Administration publishes statistics regarding how well companies do in the first ten years.[4] In their first year, 20 percent of business will fail. By year five, that number climbs to 50 percent, and when businesses hit the ten-year mark, only 30 percent of organizations will still be in business.

As organizations evolve and grow, the customers they serve also change. Natural economic cycles occur during the lifetime of a business which affect the issues that prospects face and the pain points that cause them to seek out goods and services. Technology and digital channels also change, affecting how prospects receive digital communication. Yet many organizations stick with their existing digital messaging long after the effectiveness of the message has diminished or the prospect base has shifted.

---

[4] "Do economic or industry factors affect business survival?" Small Business Administration Office of Advocacy Small Business Facts, June 2012. Accessed February 26, 2019. https://www.sba.gov/sites/default/files/Business-Survival.pdf.

During these shifts in economic climate, company evolution, and audience changes, companies can sometimes continue to maintain market share, and it may seem as though the threat of digital disengagement has receded. This, however, can be the calm before the digital storm.

Staying Proactive In Your Digital Engagement

Providing digital messaging to an audience is almost like being on a first date with the audience member every time. The expectations are high; even the smallest misstep can throw off the entire interaction. If a company is serious about securing loyal customers and brand ambassadors, digital engagement should be considered every time content is sent out into the digital universe.

There is always some change that may threaten the engagement an organization provides to customers. If there isn't a new competitor doing something innovative and original with content and delivery, there is a change in the economy or what a given customer sees as the solution to his or her problem or need. A constant state of flux provides simultaneous opportunities for new engagement and opportunities for engagement erosion. These opportunities are in essence two sides of the same coin. The side of the coin an organization falls on will be determined by how proactive the organization is with staying on its digital message.

A Brand's Digital Discovery Point

Looking back even twenty years ago, brands were introduced through traditional marketing channels such as radio, television, and direct mail. Today, a consumer brand is launched mainly in a digital space. In 2017, *Business Wire* published the results of a survey that found three out of four consumers purchase products they discover on social channels.[5] Social content is the new advertisement and purchasing agent.

Susan is a mother of two teenage children and her husband travels for work. As she flips through her Facebook feed to see what her friends are up to, she notices a good friend from high school has shared something interesting. It is a video about luggage.

Several things catch her attention at the same time. First, her friend has shared the video on this new product, and has added a comment on how this luggage is the perfect carry-on.

Second, the video showcases how a traveler can pack nearly twice as many items into the luggage due to the design and function. She typically helps her husband pack for his trips, and this luggage has each compartment clearly labeled, providing a process for packing.

---

[5] "New Survey from Curalate Finds 76% of Consumers Purchase Products They Discover on Social Media, across All Social Channels." Business Wire. November 15, 2017. Accessed February 26, 2019. https://www.businesswire.com/news/home/20171115006040/en/New-Survey-Curalate-Finds-76-Consumers-Purchase.

Lastly, the video shows how easily the luggage goes into an overhead bin. She thinks about how much faster her husband would be able to get out of the airport if he carried on his luggage versus checking it. While she may not have been in the market for a new suitcase, she clicks on the link to review the price point and return policy to see if this is something she may purchase.

Consumers will discover, assess, and investigate further or dismiss a brand in the time it takes to scroll through a social media feed. With less and less time to capture prospects' attention, let alone move them to the next stage of the conversion cycle, the digital discovery point is as sharp and small as the head of a pin.

In the example above, the time from discovery of the video on Susan's feed from her friend to clicking on the link of the ad barely spanned the length of the video in the ad. Does she need a new suitcase? That question is almost irrelevant. The digital messaging provided a story that Susan was able to consume, understand and apply.

This small window of engagement makes getting digital messages *right* more critical than ever. Brands, and their digital messages, provide key moments for prospects to discover them, versus actively searching for a product or service. These moments provide powerful inspiration and awakening in consumers and can drive new ecommerce sales for businesses.

Room To Grow

In 2018, Hootsuite shared statistics curated on digital space penetration.[6] Global social channel saturation is at 42 percent; in a nutshell, not even half of the total population is active on social channels yet. Moving to the category of active mobile social users, the percentage drops to 39 percent. With so many people yet to join the digital conversation worldwide, social channel messaging will continue to change and evolve, as will the technology providing access.

With so many new users poised to enter the digital space, experts predict that social advertisement budgets will double in the next five years. Digital messaging will become saturated; the need for strong and concise digital content will be at an all-time high.

Digital messaging is rapidly moving into a critical phase in which good habits around digital messaging will produce stronger digital engagement, and therefore better overall digital health. This is the time to develop those habits and prepare for changes that are already approaching.

---

[6] Cooper, Paige. "Social Media Advertising Stats that Matter to Marketers in 2018." Hootsuite Social Media Management. June 06, 2018. Accessed February 26, 2019. https://blog.hootsuite.com/social-media-advertising-stats/.

Chapter 3

Setting Up Your Digital House

The expression "get your house in order" is Biblical in origin. As recorded in 2 Kings, King Hezekiah of Judah (whose reign archaeological findings date to approximately 715–686 BCE) was warned by the Lord God to get his "house in order" because of an impending day of judgment. Getting his house in order became a priority for King Hezekiah, and the king enacted sweeping reforms.

If someone gets their house in order, this means they arrange their affairs and solve their problems. Sometimes this means making some tremendous decisions.

Often in business, we hear the expression that a company needs to put its financial house in order. But what about other parts of the house?

An organization's digital house is as important as any other part of the organization. My warning to you is this:

It is time to get your digital house in order.

Just as a company cannot sell products or services that are dysfunctional or not of top quality, a company cannot allow communications with prospects to be subpar or untimely and still maintain strong engagement that leads to loyal customers. A constant focus on the *quality* of digital communication is key. Quality control and monitoring of digital assets can often become a low priority for organizations, even when they state they understand the importance of good interactions.

Many times, the executive team looks at digital marketing as items on a checklist. Instead of looking at what *connection* is created with a digital asset, they focus on the asset itself. With that misplacement of focus, a brand's reputation and message can easily be damaged.

The Digital Phoenix Rising

Before a guided tour of how to improve your digital marketing, I'd like you to meet your tour guide. My name is Lisa Apolinski, and I run a digital consulting agency named 3 Dog Write. This is our organization's origin story.

In January 2013, I was sitting in my hotel room in Milan, having returned very late from a long, grueling day at work. I was on the phone with my sister, venting about my challenging day.

"I was verbally raked over the coals again by my boss because I don't have content to create that new product brochure. It isn't like I don't know *how* to develop a brochure, but creating one with no key selling points will not get anyone *interested*."

"And haven't you done a ton of work to make their digital message strong?"

"Well, at least I can demonstrate best practices for brand strategy with my side work. There, at least, I get to make a real difference."

"Let me ask you then: How does working your side job make you feel?"

"I feel like a superhero, and I am actually listened to."

"So, why are you putting all this energy into someone else's company? Why not make that side job your full-time job and invest in your own future?"

With that phone call, my sister posed a question that forever changed the course of my career and my life. That moment spurred my rebirth into the corporate world, from the position of employee to strategic advisor and digital engagement expert at the helm of my own digital consulting agency.

I am just like you: I have to run a company, keep up with changes in digital engagement, and manage how my clients respond to my brand. Reviewing my digital message keeps my own communication authentic and applicable. And like you, I have to constantly work for the engagement I have with my audience. If I don't, they will go elsewhere, and they will go in a nanosecond.

All companies have to work diligently to keep up with changes in how their prospects communicate with them and receive their messaging. The digital world is fluid and has a great amount of power, like a wave crashing on a shoreline. But many companies underestimate the impact of that world on their revenue and continued prosperity.

Slow But Still Strong

Changes in digital engagement oftentimes are slow in progression and therefore can be even slower to detect. Once the engagement has started to shift, there are opportunities to pick up on the movement and modify digital messaging to keep digital engagement strong with prospects and customers.

Even now, many companies, because of our current economic state, are doing well despite a less-than-strong digital presence. And going along as business-as-usual in a strong economy for many organizations allows a reasonable revenue stream. Good economic times, however, offer a perfect environment to review and begin to test new potential markets, new audiences, and new digital engagement.

Company leaders may also think that, since digital communication worked in the past, there is no reason to change the engagement, even in the face of data that shows changes in purchasing behavior or a progression of the conversion cycle.

As new technology is used by prospects, the conversion cycle will also change, or progress, to accommodate these new behaviors. Email is a great example of how a conversion cycle can progress.

When email was first used, the communication was strictly business to business. As households added a computer and internet connection, businesses discovered a new digital communication tool to prospects through email. Subject lines were not reviewed or even tested (via open rates) when emails were first being sent. Today, companies conduct testing of subject lines to determine the best three to five words. Digital communication should evolve because your prospects' needs will evolve over time, as will the ways in which prospects want to receive digital communication.

Not only is there more room for companies to test and fail digital engagement during prosperous times, there are also more potential prospects available to test with new digital targeting. Again, this engagement feedback and testing takes time. But during a strong economy, testing and targeting can be added to gain valuable insight that can be applied when an organization needs stronger engagement in a short amount of time.

The Digital Show Is Never Completed

Does this mean that in economic downturns, or in times when a company is not seeing strong profits, the opportunity for digital testing has passed? Not at all. There is always opportunity and experiences that can be created, even in some of the worst of times.

During economic uncertainty, some organizational leaders may feel they need to shrink away from marketing to preserve market share. During the 2008 recession, I witnessed nearly whole marketing departments cut, and their budgets with them. They may believe that somehow, by hunkering down and stopping digital engagement, they will weather the storm until it passes. Prospects and customers, however, still want to experience digital communication and engagement, no matter the situation.

Companies do not *shrink to success* in any aspect. Shrinking a company's digital presence when it has taken a long time to develop and establish that presence creates opportunities for competitors to fill in that digital void.

And there is always a new competitor ready to occupy that digital space.

In both times of economic growth and economic downturns, the constant should be digital engagement, but the message will change as the economy and prospects' needs change. Seek to first understand how prospects are communicated with, the timing of the communication, and every way a prospect receives communication through a process review.

Diligence Through A Process Review

Organizations can conduct several exercises to stay on top of prospect engagement details. A first step is to perform a channel discovery review. Such a review can take a couple of days and requires representatives from every department with which a prospect will engage; the information it reveals can be enlightening. By going through every means through which a prospect engages with an organization (for example, digital engagement, phone engagement, direct mail, etc.), any changes in technology or potential gaps in communication become clear.

This process can be instructive and the information gained is often surprising. By mapping out the entire engagement and conversion process, assumptions are forced into the light. Organizations may uncover sections skipped in a conversion cycle that were unknown before. They may uncover how staff members in a given department do not follow communication protocols with prospects. They may even discover assumptions that underlie how prospects find information necessary to decide how to become a customer. Once a process is documented and optimized, data can come into play.

Staying On Track With Data

With digital channels, there is ample opportunity to capture data to better understand who is engaged with digital content and how those individuals reached digital content.

Data should be tracked and reviewed each month to learn more about the audience that has been engaging with various digital communications, including the company's website, digital ads, and social media. At minimum, review how audiences come into a digital channel, if there are new geographic areas or industries engaging with digital content, or if there are new followers on a digital channel.

Based on the data trends discovered each month, customer personas can be developed to create a detailed visual of each new group potentially engaging with digital content.

The Development Of Customer Personas

Customer personas should include an age range, location, job title, industry identification, and what the person might be looking for with digital content.

As an example of a customer persona looking for a digital consulting agency, Linda is a fifty-two-year-old chief marketing officer who lives in Austin, Texas. She has been in marketing for her entire career, and is having a hard time keeping up with new social channels and how they might work with the prospects she engages in the financial industry.

With this level of persona detail, digital messaging can be developed, tested and tracked to see how well engagement is received. By having a company's ideal customer developed, when communication is created, content can be written specifically for that persona. For a writer, developing content for Linda provides an anchor specifically to her needs. An article that gives the top ten ways to use Facebook for finance clients would be much more appealing to Linda than an article that discusses how college students are using Twitter.

Time Will Tell

No matter where an organization is in its life cycle and no matter what the economic climate, there is still time to observe and learn about your customers and prospects.

The kinds of content that create an impact and how that content is discovered and consumed have already changed. Time will provide the space companies need to uncover new channels, new ways to engage, and new consumers of their content.

During strong economic health, organizations need to develop content that matters—content that can cut through digital noise or digital obstacles. As data is tracked and information is gathered, companies can learn a great deal about the customers they have captured and the customers they wish to gain in the future.

Customers will have different purchasing patterns depending on the economic climate. With that information, companies can also see how, during times of different economic patterns, the consumption of content also changes, which may involve increases, decreases, or portions of content seeing higher engagement rates, with other portions never being read.

With preparation and testing of new messages, companies can obtain a better understanding of their current customer journey and how customers purchase during both economic good times and bad.

Think of this time as a mystery waiting to be revealed. Data and content engagement will reveal further secrets on the motivations of customers to purchase or not. These data points provide vital information to both your current customer engagement and your future prospect engagement opportunities.

Where We Are Headed

Wasting valuable data is equivalent to tossing out requests for products and services or not showing up to customer appointments. If a company truly wants to see how to properly engage customers, taking the time to review and put the digital house in order must be a top priority.

So, what steps does an organization need to take in order to see that the digital house is ready and prepped for the road ahead? How can the digital house be ready if change is inevitable? Key areas provide the foundation for the house to be sturdy and ready for any storm that may come.

The foundation starts before digital channels are even launched. Discover what specific steps an organization should take to set up its digital house so the house does not get blown in. At the end of each subsequent chapter is a box labeled Guarding The Digital Fortress summarizing key takeaways to help safeguard your digital house.

Chapter 4

Mastering Data Application

As I sat at dinner, a colleague named Jane relayed a story and asked me for my opinion. During the course of just three months, a social media channel account for one of Jane's clients had doubled its number of likes.

"It may be my suspicion, but a new marketer started, and suddenly there was a large uptick in likes for the page," said Jane.

"What does your client think?" I asked.

"The initial reaction was that the number of likes was a very good thing," said Jane. "More means better, right?"

When I dug a little deeper, I found something that could cause an issue in the long term.

Data Beware: A Cautionary Tale

Jane had reason to be suspicious. Those likes were gained through a paid ad campaign specifically for the purposes of gaining new likes. That is not necessarily an issue in itself; the issue was in the additional data points that I discovered. The majority of new likes, which were now nearly 65 percent of the total likes, came from countries notorious for large click farms (dedicated teams of individuals who like pages and are paid based on number of likes). In addition, these countries were not among the client's targets, nor would they be targeted in the near future. Comparing the likes of this page to those of similar companies, the number of likes was almost double what some of the most popular competitor pages had.

The bigger issue has to do with content *engagement*. Many social media channels continually modify their algorithm, serving content to a viewer's feed based on engagement statistics. If content is being viewed, commented on, shared, and liked, that content is offered to more people in the network. When click farms come into play, those individuals will never engage with content from the hundreds, if not thousands, of pages they have liked. In many instances, click farms generate likes from fabricated accounts that are used exclusively to like pages—not to engage.

When the majority of likes on a company page are due to phony accounts or accounts for which the individual is not actually a member of the target audience, the activity on the company's content decreases. When the activity decreases, the content is not offered up to other page members who actually *would* engage with it. Think of this as a field with flowers, but those flowers are surrounded by weeds. It is much harder to see the flowers due to all the weeds that obstruct the view.

Content engagement for my colleague's client was already experiencing diminishing returns because of this influx in questionable likes on the page. One data point was the focus, but it affected other digital areas. So, what drove this decision to purchase likes versus allowing organic growth?

The answer was something other companies have experienced in this digital age. Board members wanted to see more likes on the social media channels because of a common point of view: More likes on a page means more engagement. In theory, that is a sound argument. But in reality, the way the likes were gained actually hurt overall engagement.

I was asked by my colleague how the client could remedy this digital misstep.

The first step would be to educate the board on what data points mean and don't mean. Allowing time and space for organic growth in likes, in the long run, can make a digital channel stronger and more of a community for those who are on the channel. The second step is much harder. Each like that was suspect would need to be examined individually to see if the account looked fake, and each fake like needed to be removed. The issue was not that every fake like would be removed, but those truly interested in the page could potentially also be removed in the process.

The page on this social channel had been slowly grown and built for many years, and within a matter of ten or so weeks, that growth and engagement had been severely compromised by one decision based on changing one data point—just one data point! This is a data application error.

Are Data Points Good Or Bad?

Data capture and data application are two sides of the same coin. The first step of our digital house overhaul is to understand what data we are capturing and why.

Metrics are different for different channels, but the idea is the same. Based on the data being captured, there is an assumption of behavior. For example, *website inbound traffic* may show initial interest and access to a website. *Bounce rate* on a given page shows movement to another channel or digital asset.

Data application uses data metrics to develop hypotheses regarding consumer behavior, including how engaged or not engaged someone is with a particular piece of digital content. The discipline uses a point of view to develop a theory on engagement behavior. It is important with data application to be aware of any biases and modify digital assets to uncover these potential biases that may cloud the interpretation.

Data metric development and data application are critical to optimizing digital assets and spotting new engagement behavior so the user experience is always enhanced and on point. While some believe strong data engagement metrics are the only metrics to have, metrics that show disengagement can be just as powerful, allowing missteps in digital content to be corrected. What does *not* work can provide as much insight as what *does* work. Why do so many companies want to inflate strong numbers to always show positive engagement?

When Data Is Misused

Metrics around digital engagement, and subsequently data application, are a hot topic and quite controversial. Marketing guru Rand Fishkin has commented on the inaccuracy of one of the largest online advertising platforms: Google AdWords (https://moz.com/blog/unreliable-google-adwords-keyword-volume), going so far as to say relying on keyword volume numbers from Google is insane.

Facebook has been sued by smaller advertisers that the video ad metrics have been inflated in order to attract more advertisers.[7] The statistic that Facebook was applying was around number of minutes that individuals watch a video—a seemingly straightforward data point.

The calculation of the average duration of a video being watched did not factor in video engagement that lasted less than three seconds. This is a key point of data—viewers who are not interested in or engaged with video content abandon videos within three to four seconds after starting.

The philosophy that metrics should be modified to show only strong engagement come from an assumption that data is good or bad. It is neither. Data simply *is*. Understanding how audiences engage with content has power in and of itself.

Understand Points Of View On Data

Returning to the data points mentioned above, website traffic and bounce rate: Assume Company X has suddenly seen a tremendous increase in website traffic. In fact, the increase has come over several weeks and there

---

[7] "Facebook is Sued for 'inflating' Ad Watch Times by up to 900% to Lure in Advertisers." RT International. October 17, 2018. Accessed February 26, 2019. https://www.rt.com/usa/441569-facebook-inflated-video-numbers.

has been no announcement or news from the company that would explain an increase in website traffic. While an increase in website traffic is something a company wants, the assumption is increased traffic equates to increased brand awareness and prospect connecting.

The alert marketer will dig further to see how the website traffic is coming in. Is it coming from a new referral source? If so, is it a referral source that should be explored, perhaps by adding digital content to that channel or website source? Is it an expected referral source because of an article that was recently published?

Is the new traffic coming from a country or city where the company does business? If not, is it an emerging market or is it a known area where click farms operate? By reviewing where the new website traffic is coming from, many new questions can be posed and tested.

Bounce rate indicates when a visitor navigates *away* from a given page. Typically, before a bounce, the visitor has viewed a single page. Many may consider a high bounce rate as negative; however, if a blog has been shared on a social media channel, typical behavior would be to go to the page, read it, and then exit and continue on the social media feed. A better indicator of engagement would be how many access and, if possible, how long these visitors stay on the site, which would indicate if they read the content or quickly exited. In this instance, bounce rate would not provide any further information on engagement, but *length of time* on the page would.

Understanding data metrics and data application can also help guide both the marketer and the executive team to make better digital decisions. It is imperative as digital experts to educate others on the significance of key data points and to point out misinformed data application.

Applying Data Wisely

There are so many data points to track; where should an organization begin? Key areas can be reviewed and from there, relevant areas for data tracking will unfold. Consider these applications the tip of the digital iceberg. Once these questions are answered, other questions will rise to the surface that demand to be answered through data.

- **Where are visitors coming from?** This includes referral traffic and country of origin.

- **What page do visitors hit first?** Visitors can arrive via any page, including the home page, internal pages, or the contact page.

- **How long do they stay on the main page?** Apply the ten:ten rule. Traffic that stays for either too short a duration (under ten seconds) or too long (over ten minutes) should be classified as suspect.

- **What is their digital journey?** Being able to follow visitors' paths through digital assets can shed light on their odyssey to understanding the organization's message.

- **What is the bounce rate and where is the exit point?** Bounce rate has a context, so be sure to apply that context. And the exit point within the digital asset shows when a visitor is ready to move on.

Data application is like solving a murder mystery. Instead of looking for potential clues (data points), the digital detective discovers more about the visitor's digital journey. Just like a murder mystery, certain data points are applicable, while some can take an organization off track. Familiarity with a company's data provides valuable insight into prospects and future engagement trends.

Setting up digital engagement through proper technology usage is the natural progression from data application. The next chapter discusses this important, and often overlooked, topic.

Guarding The Digital Fortress

There are steps an organization can take for understanding data points and making data application work.

1. **Understand your data points.** What do data points mean and what do they not mean for digital engagement? What significance do executives or other individuals put on select data points?

2. **Put data into context.** This can be the hardest point to master. A data point without context is simply a number. Look at the how to understand the why.

3. **Dig deeper into your data.** One data point should never dictate strategy (as the cautionary tale above illustrates). A deeper picture of digital engagement can be found when additional data is added to the story.

4. **Get into the habit of reporting.** Get into the habit of looking at data in reports. A good rule of thumb is to pull weekly reports and set up comparisons (week over week, year over year) so data can be tracked easily and trends can be seen early.

5. **Compare the data.** Benchmark comparison to other industry competitors can help an organization to not fall into the trap of falling in love with their own data. Comparisons can also help with understanding digital channel metrics and what is considered an average or above-average metric mark.

6. **Take control.** The best thing an organization can do is to take control and understand its own data. No one will understand an organization's data better than the organization—including industry nuances and changes in the economic environment that affects digital engagement.

Chapter 5

Using Technology Wisely

My next client, Perry, came to ask for help with updating the company website. The website had been developed in the late 1990s, which at the time did not have to worry about mobile display and development. The website was dated, but more importantly, had been developed using an old way of thinking.

When websites were still in this infant stage of use, many marketers used the term "above the fold," meaning the first section of a website users saw before scrolling. During this time, marketers focused on creating the best content in this prime real estate. Any content placed below the fold was less important, as the consensus was that content in that area would not be seen with any consistency.

Not Your Mom's Website

When Perry's website was developed back in the '90s, nobody owned smartphones. With the adoption of mobile devices, scrolling is now a natural and expected behavior, so the concept of placing the best or most important content above the fold is no longer applicable. In fact, scrolling is expected today and is used in many social channels, including Facebook and Twitter.

Because of changes in technology and how users access digital content, websites have adapted, becoming cleaner, simpler, and longer, following user behavior of scrolling for additional content. Instead of websites being designed horizontally, with many subpages (in alignment with keeping content above the fold), websites are now vertically designed with few subpages and a much more streamlined navigational structure.

By modifying this client's website to be mobile-friendly and to work with scrolling behavior, content was better distributed and navigation simplified for easier access and engagement. Traffic and website page engagement increased as much as 40 percent on certain pages for this particular client.

Technology Times, They Are A-Changin'

Before the introduction of the mobile phone, the methods companies employed to get messages to their prospects and customers were limited, consisting primarily of mail, radio ads, and television ads. Today, according to *Business Insider*, two-thirds of the world's population is connected by mobile devices.[8] That correlates to just over five billion people. With the ability to access limitless prospects at any time in any location, technology has revolutionized how organizations provide content to their prospects and customers.

Many organizations consider digital content a priority but do not always consider how that digital content is delivered. Technology is a key component for optimizing digital engagement and the user experience. Technology is also key for staff operations, to ensure accuracy and fast turnaround within the conversion process.

By focusing on the use of technology in every aspect of engagement, companies can take control of the technology experience instead of allowing technology to dictate the experience. Both the internal and external use of technology impact the user experience, so both can be optimized for maximum leverage.

Understanding Technology At An Early Age

When I was little, my father used to bring me along when he would purchase new equipment for the drugstore he ran. During one particular outing, he was purchasing a new cash register that had to be plugged in because it

---

[8] Hollander, Rayna. "Two-thirds of the World's Population Are Now Connected by Mobile Devices." Business Insider. September 19, 2017. Accessed February 27, 2019. https://www.businessinsider.com/world-population-mobile-devices-2017-9.

had a small computer inside. This new technology was very bulky, but allowed for transactions to be tracked; a printout could be produced at the end of each cashier's shift to reconcile the drawer with the printout.

I was left with the new cash register and I did what any child does—I played with the register. What I did not realize during the time I was left with the register was that I was training myself to understand the distinct features of the new technology.

When my father and the seller came back into the room, my father asked how a report was generated. While the seller flipped through the very large manual, I was able to quickly demonstrate how, since I had already discovered several fun features on this novel device.

Internal Workings Of Technology

When I was brought in for a training assignment only a few years ago, I observed the inside sales department of a large organization in the Los Angeles area. I was surprised that many of the operations and sales processing relied on paper and manual entries, even though more than 60 percent of prospects accessed information through the company's website.

One main module that had not yet been activated and linked to Outlook by IT was a feature to create communication templates based on where the prospect was in the conversion cycle, linking communication to the prospect's CRM (customer relationship management) database entry. The company had paid for the module and had not been able to access the module because this last step had yet to be implemented.

Once the module was linked in Outlook, the organization realized several key results. First, all communication with prospects was finally populated in the CRM and retained in digital form for each prospect, showing exactly what communication had been sent and when. This allowed anyone in the organization to run a report to see prior communications and thereby evaluate prospects' progression through the conversion cycle. Second, by having templates that all sales associates could use, the time sales staff needed to draft communications with prospects was greatly reduced. Lastly, digital communications could be tested, optimized, and made consistent for all prospects.

So Many Features Not Being Used

As with many companies I have worked with in the past, this company used a well-established CRM (customer relationship management) software package with standard modules. And like many other companies, these modules were available, paid for, and not being used.

This is a common occurrence. Organizations purchase and partially implement technology, but the full software package that is purchased can be so complex, with features so numerous and overwhelming, keeping up and keeping track becomes difficult. There are steps, however, that can be taken to optimize the technology being used in internal teams such as sales, marketing, and operations.

- **Do a digital due diligence.** A *digital process map*, such as the one created from the channel discovery review described in chapter 3, highlights areas where technology is not being used, but could benefit from having a process in place.

- **Review current technology.** Most companies pay for or have access to support on the technology package that has been purchased. Contact the support staff or sales representative of the organization's purchased or licensed technology and review everything, including each included module or feature (this may take a couple of calls). In addition, ask internal staff (including IT and all stakeholders) to contribute any questions or concerns for integrating the features into the current technology library of the company.

- **Get trained.** Master users are critical to ensure various technology packages are fully used. These highly trained individuals who work within a company understand the ins and outs of a given platform and serve as internal resources for other staff members when they have questions. Training should be done yearly to keep master users current on features of the technology. This can be initiated and accomplished by the technology company or by the master user, depending on the complexity of the technology and the material to be covered. Master users should attend official technology training every six months to stay current with changes and updates of the software.

The internal workings of an organization rely heavily on technology use to effectively process prospects through a conversion cycle. Due to time and the budgetary constraints required to add technology to a company's internal infrastructure, changes in technology are typically slow and require a careful approach.

The manner in which prospects use technology and their expectations of technology, however, can be more pronounced.

Technology Moves At Lightning Speed

Technological innovations are happening at ever-increasing speed and frequency. For instance, while the top few social channels have remained fairly steady, there are more than 200 social media platforms currently active online. According to Smart Insights, there is only a 42 percent penetration of global active social media users, which leads to the conclusion that additional social media platforms could be developed to engage these additional users.[9]

Technology and user experiences can change rapidly as well, and with those changes, behavioral expectations of how content is delivered. Take the next example as food for thought.

The Emergence Of Video

HootSuite provided some interesting statistics regarding YouTube. Every month, nearly 2 billion users visit YouTube, and every day, these users watch a billion hours of video.[10]

In the land of digital engagement, video is still being discovered and developed. Because consumption of video has not yet peaked (Google reports the average mobile viewing session lasts a little over 40 minutes, which is up 50 percent year-over-year,[11] viewers may

---

[9] Chaffey, Dave. "Global Social Media Research Summary 2019." Smart Insights. February 12, 2019. Accessed February 27, 2019. https://www.smartinsights.com/social-media-marketing/social-media-strategy/new-global-social-media-research/.

[10] Cooper, Paige. "22 YouTube Stats That Matter to Marketers in 2019." Hootsuite Social Media Management. January 23, 2019. Accessed April 14, 2019. https://blog.hootsuite.com/youtube-stats-marketers/.

[11] Miners, Zach. "The Average Mobile YouTube Session Is Now 40 Minutes, Google Says." CIO. July 16, 2015. Accessed April 14, 2019. http://www.cio.com/article/2949473/the-average-mobile-youtube-session-is-now-40-minutes-google-says.html.

be more forgiving of missteps, and the data points that indicate a strong video arrive quickly (if a video is not engaging or about what was advertised, viewers will exit within ten seconds of a video starting).

The other interesting facet of YouTube is international access. YouTube is accessible in nearly eighty different languages, covering approximately 95 percent of viewers online. As markets become more competitive, companies will need to establish international reach in order to grow.

Companies can make sure they check off a few easy engagement optimization steps with their YouTube channel:

- **Use of tags.** YouTube is the second-largest search engine after Google (and is in fact owned by Google). Because of this, *tags* are available to assist with not only search by viewers, but also with what video content is offered up after a viewer watches a particular video. Tag usage is key to searchable video content.

- **Closed captioning.** Many video viewers watch in locations where the sound is muted. Be sure to add closed captioning to video—an inexpensive and easy process. Many companies are now available to do closed captioning with fast turnaround and high accuracy.

- **Not lost in translation.** If an organization identifies viewers (and therefore prospects) from other countries viewing video content, adding closed captioning in additional languages can assist with enhanced engagement.

The Digital Journey Is Not A Linear One

When prospects and customers engage with a company's digital assets, the journey is frequently not a straight path, but a series of starts and stops, direction changes, and detours. Part of the reason a digital journey is so fragmented is because of the different devices that provide access to content.

As additional changes continue to unfold with technology, so too will users' expectations of the digital content experience. So, what steps can an organization take to stay abreast of new technology, especially when changes are emerging rapidly?

Guarding The Digital Fortress

Not every new technology makes sense for every organization. Companies can and should be discerning of what technology is added to digital engagement. Many new technologies simply may not apply to an organization's customer base or make sense with how its customers access digital content. By understanding how a company's digital footprint is discovered by prospects, new and emerging technology can be evaluated to see whether and how it enhances the user experience.

With data tracking in place and the technological method of delivery optimized, digital content can be created for strong engagement. Make sure you take the following steps:

1. **Be the content consumer.** Staff members at organizations are practicing the behaviors that are emerging with prospects. As new behavior changes how your employees access content, consider how that new behavior affects customers and prospects.

2. **Identify the geek squad.** Many organizations have staff members who are early adopters of technology. Be sure to identify those individuals, and have monthly or quarterly meetings where these individuals can share what new technology or digital channels are emerging.

3. **Hit the trade show floor.** Conference and trade shows like the Consumer Electronic Show, EmTech Asia, and SXSW highlight where technology is going. Make attending shows on technology trends and innovations part of employee professional development.

Chapter 6

Digital Engagement and Re-engagement

B *rand story review* is not an item simply to check off a list. There is a digital storm approaching, and it is forming on different sides.

There is more content being created than can be consumed by a digital audience. BrandWatch estimates that on WordPress alone, nearly 75 million blog posts are published every month.[12] And Nielsen estimates that in the United States, adults interact with some kind of media at least half of their day, just over eleven hours.[13]

Preparing For The Digital Storm Ahead

The inversion of available content versus consumption has digital information consumers at a crisis point. Mark

---

[12] Smith, Kit. "122 Amazing Social Media Statistics and Facts." Brandwatch. Accessed February 27, 2019. https://www.brandwatch.com/blog/amazing-social-media-statistics-and-facts/.

[13] "Time Flies: U.S. Adults Now Spend Nearly Half a Day Interacting with Media." What People Watch, Listen To and Buy. Accessed February 27, 2019. https://www.nielsen.com/us/en/insights/news/2018/time-flies-us-adults-now-spend-nearly-half-a-day-interacting-with-media.html.

Schaefer discussed this idea of content shock as hitting a tipping point in 2014, where free digital content is doubling every nine to twenty-four months.[14] However, there is a limit to the time available to consume digital content. With so much content and so little time, even strong content is having a difficult time finding engagement.

Digital readers are becoming more and more discerning regarding what content they consume, and even more so on what content they share. The concept of loyal followers has also fallen by the wayside. A research study by Media Post indicates that millennials show less brand loyalty (only 29 percent) than Gen X.[15] And Gen X brand loyalty only applies to one in three people.

On the other side, as of the writing of this book, while nobody has an economic crystal ball, many business analysts are predicting a recession in the next few years, some even saying it will happen within the next several months. Consumers purchase during recessions, but the behavior and rationale for purchasing changes during such times. And while the recession of 2007–2009 can provide some information on what drives purchasing behavior during an economic downturn, the future may or may not follow that same behavioral pattern.

[14] "Content Shock: Why Content Marketing Is Not a Sustainable Strategy." Schaefer Marketing Solutions: We Help Businesses {grow}. November 29, 2017. Accessed April 14, 2019. https://businessesgrow.com/2014/01/06/content-shock/.

[15] Loechner, Jack. "Brand Loyalty Not A Millennial Trait." Mediapost.com. March 20, 2018. Accessed February 27, 2019. https://www.mediapost.com/publications/article/316190/brand-loyalty-not-a-millennial-trait.html.

Marketers must overcome several obstacles in digital engagement: digital content overload, reduced attention spans, lack of brand loyalty, economic upheaval, behavioral changes in content consumption based on new technology. The list seems to go on and on. By focusing on the foundation of digital engagement and brand content, the marketer can work with and through these obstacles.

The Fight For Five Seconds

The marketing industry touts conventional wisdom that consumers have declining attention spans. In fact, Cision has researched and discovered that an average viewer of digital content has an attention span of less than eight seconds.[16] A content consumer decides very quickly whether to stay on a current piece of digital content or to move on.

With content being consumed (and/or encountered and discarded) at unprecedented speed, companies have only seconds to capture a prospect's eye and attention. Companies are then asking for prospects to engage with that content with shares, comments, and likes—asking for even more engagement time.

---

[16] "Are Declining Attention Spans Killing Your Content Marketing Strategy?" cision.com January 22, 2018. Accessed February 27, 2019. https://www.cision.com/us/2018/01/declining-attention-killing-content-marketing-strategy/.

With so much competition in the digital world for bandwidth and attention, many organizations surprisingly do not keep their brand story current or optimize their brand story for constant and consistent engagement. Content and brand stories that are not refreshed and built upon lose engagement quickly and lose the momentum of the digital race.

Brand Reimagined

When my next client requested assistance, this large organization in the hospitality industry was not asking for brand boosting or modification. They had requested simple content creation to engage clients who might stay at their property. Here is the idea this client had: If an organization kept pumping out content, that was good enough to keep engagement going. The content that was shared was factual but not inspirational: specials on rooms or the spa or additions to staff. Brand fortification was not even within the realm of thought, yet was a vital component of this digital content situation.

The one piece of the brand puzzle that was missing for this property was an authentic narrative, something that could be summed up in less than one minute. The estate had been in the family for over a century and was converted into a multiple room property so visitors could experience and enjoy the area, known for hiking and amazing scenery.

When staff members were interviewed on what made this hotel property different, however, each shared a different view, much like the proverbial blind men who each touched a part of the elephant and described what they were experiencing. Even though each perspective could resonate with a particular guest, a full narrative would be much more compelling for someone staying at the property. This included the history of the area, the estate and the desire of the family to bring visitors to the area and experience all the area has to offer.

Because the current brand story did not deliver an authentic and emotional moment to prospects, the brand was slowly but surely losing market share. And because of the varying brand stories being created by staff, content was not consistent, which led to a "fake" feeling for potential guests.

The client had to go back to basics and rediscover why the owners had decided to create this property in the first place. What was the defining moment that caused this property to come into being? How did that moment define the brand and key differentiators of the property?

With that new (and at the same time, old) brand story discovered, the next step was to re-engage and share the authentic brand message both internally and externally. The property worked to re-evaluate and edit every piece of communication, from digital to print to internal messaging and graphics. But the message became very clear: This is why we exist, and this is what we stand for every day for our guests, and why our guests should stay with us at our property versus another location.

By establishing a core brand story, creating engaging content that built from that foundation was seamless. It was no longer the struggle it had been. With staff all on the same brand page, digital content creation and sharing became more genuine, and more staff members were able to contribute to the digital story. New digital content created engagement and transformation for the employees, and prospects were able to identify that engagement shift and respond in a positive way to that shift.

Similarly, guests were also inspired to share their visit on the property's social media channels, and added to the digital content from the guest perspective. These impromptu shares provided other prospects with ideas on staying at the property.

Brand Foundation Brings Strength

One factor that has been shown to level the playing field and assist in the fortification process is time. Time is still on the side of the brand marketer. Instead of focusing on intensity, the marketer should focus on consistency—in both message and frequency.

Shifting the brand story does not mean turning the ship on a dime. Rather, marketers should watch for icebergs ahead and start to navigate around those obstacles. The concept of the brand foundation in a digital approach almost sounds counterintuitive. Digital engagement moves so fast, so why not simply change the brand story radically?

Digital engagement can move quickly, but the human factor must also be taken into account. A dramatic shift in brand story that feels forced or generated could alienate digital audiences. Taking the time to go back to the brand emergence story and also to understand what the brand means to current audiences will help marketers find a story that captures attention and stays grounded in current understanding and expectations.

Let Go Of The Viral Dream

I have been asked by several companies how they can produce *one piece* of digital content and make that content go viral. Many companies still cling to the idea that a single piece of viral content (blog, press release, video, image) will make all of their website traffic woes and lack of brand recognition go away.

Again, consider the disparity of intensity versus consistency. While having a piece of content that goes viral seems ideal, viral content is not sustainable. In 2013, a girl created a dancing video in which she quit her job. She danced her way through an empty office, sound room and even bathroom. (https://www.youtube.com/watch?v=MS4n84a2Mw4)

If someone was asked what country she was from or what she did for a living, many probably would not know. But the video did go viral, with almost a quarter-million views, which was impressive for that time period. She was offered a job by Queen Latifah at her talk show, and that show was cancelled the following year.

Interest in a company's brand story and dedication to an organization's digital content is a series of small wins built up over time. By demonstrating a consistent strategy for engagement and purposeful investment of time and resources in creating meaningful and authentic content, not only are companies securing followers, they are providing a high-quality path for new audiences who might find them later on.

Keeping Your Digital Assets Secure

One final item needs to be reviewed annually to keep digital asset management a top priority: who has access to a company's digital channels. When organizations bring in consultants, agencies, new employees, interns, and anyone else to the digital house, these guests are provided access—a set of keys—to those channels.

When those individuals leave, many companies forget to remove access to those digital channels.

At the start of each year, companies can and should create an access security process. Take just a few minutes to change passwords, remove outdated access to social channels, and audit website admin access. Not only does this simple step remove the possibility of a disgruntled individual blowing up a company's brand, this step also puts ownership of the digital assets back where they belong: in the hands of the organization.

Picking Members For Your Digital Team

While this book talks about different aspects of digital asset management and engagement, there is an underlying theme: people. Content is not created in a vacuum and neither is content consumed in a vacuum. Content is created for people by people.

With the complexity of digital engagement and technology, companies will bring in consultants to support, assist, and lead. During my time in the corporate world, I have hired many consultants to assist my team. I am now on the other side of the table, and I have seen great consultants come in (along with highly questionable consultants) to provide strategy and thought leadership.

The issue I struggled with during my corporate tenure and the issue I see many organizations struggle with is choosing members of the digital team (the right people at the right time). This topic is one of the easiest to skip over in importance, yet one of the most critical points in preparing for the digital storm ahead; it is the next subject of discussion.

Guarding The Digital Fortress

Marketers can use several best practices for a strong digital content creation strategy.

1. **Show thought leadership versus selling.** The biggest mistake companies make is to go right to selling products and services. Thought leadership focuses on insights and sharing knowledge, which helps create industry experts. People like to hear from industry experts, not people who just sell.

2. **Create content your readers want, not what your company likes.** Instead of creating content that an executive team thinks is interesting, step into the mind

of the reader. What topics are of interest to the audience? What pain points are the readers having that can be addressed with digital content?

3. **Create clear next steps.** If readers have taken the time to view digital content, help them to continue their digital discovery journey. Provide links or clear next steps in digital content.

4. **Make content creation a habit.** There is no hard and fast rule on how often digital content should be created. The most important rule is to create in a consistent manner. Develop a monthly calendar and add in topics weekly to keep the conversation going.

5. **Use mixed media in your content.** Mixed media can be images, infographics, video, or audio. And this mixed media can be anywhere. I recently saw a posting for an open position; the hiring manager added a short audio clip talking about why he was looking to hire. Keep an open mind when deciding where to put mixed media in your digital content.

6. **Many hands make the digital burden light.** And many voices make the digital content interesting. There are millions of points of view, so why limit digital content to just one? Tap different departments and staff members and create content that shows the complexity of an organization along with the human factor.

7. **Put your content where people can find that content.** Content that is buried in a digital channel or not easy to find or search will not see the light of day, let alone be discovered by customers and prospects. Companies are quite good at sharing content. But when a reader wants to go back to that channel later on, make the navigation clear and let the URL help with searching for that digital content later on.

8. **Decide thoughtfully on collecting data.** I am not opposed to collecting contact information for digital content that offers a lot of information, took a long time to create or research, or offers secrets to success. But nothing can be

more irritating than providing contact info only to discover digital content that does not live up to that hype behind a gate. If there is any doubt whether to make the content free to consume, err on the side of open access.

9. **Stay authentic to your brand story.** Content themes should be clear to feel authentic to a brand. Suddenly talking about baking when a company sells insurance feels out of step and a weird attempt at humanizing the content. Stay in the vein of the brand story with digital content. Save baking recipes for personal posts.

10. **Focus on the conversation instead of being in the right.** Many marketers feel compelled either to defend or to remain opinion-free with digital content. By focusing on empowering conversation, all sides of the conversation can be heard without judgment.

Chapter 7

Identifying Who Could Hurt Your Digital Fortification

A large organization had brought on a few different agencies, mine included, to assist with digital marketing growth. I always enjoy the opportunity to collaborate with new agencies, and I welcomed the chance to do so in this case. What I discovered was that not all agencies are equal.

Here was the fatal flaw: There were strategies executed without discussion by one agency that affected more than digital engagement. These strategic decisions started to impact website traffic and ultimately conversion. Yet the agency in question kept on implementing decisions without so much as a backwards glance to consider the digital carnage left in its wake.

What Are You Really Asking For In Your Team?

While I wish there was a happy ending to this story, I can share the reality: The agency still works with this company and is still affecting its strategy and digital engagement, sometimes good and sometimes bad.

Because of this experience, my agency has become a specialist in restoration consulting for digital engagement strategy. This is a specialty practice that reverses damage or restores a strong and appropriate digital strategy when an internal staff member was in over his or her head, or an inappropriate or ill-fitting consultant was placed in the digital driver's seat.

Being asked to come into an organization to undo damage is becoming more commonplace in the consulting world. There are more and more consultants, and while some are brilliant and ethical, some are simply not. Yet companies invite these people into their digital house, and in some cases, let them move in. In the digital strategy space, the below four categories of hires can be engagement killers. Each type has a unique ability to derail strategy.

With all the talk of digital engagement, the human factor can easily be overlooked. Who provides strategic guidance is an important determiner of success for a given digital engagement strategy. And there are four types of people—staff, executives and consultants—who can destroy digital engagement faster than digital copy can be developed.

The Know-It-All

The Know-It-All presents a front: always having the answer. While confidence is great, thinking that someone knows, or has, all the answers is unrealistic. This mentality provides no opportunity for learning and growth.

Digital engagement is rapidly changing, and particular strategies that work well today could be significantly less effective tomorrow. By believing s/he has all the answers, The Know-It-All gets boxed in. Even new data or industry changes do not deter the cockiness of The Know-It-All.

When questioned on new tactics or technology, The Know-It-All will brush off new information, or worse, attack the individual questioning. The attack feels personal to The Know-It-All, who feels the need to defend rather than listen.

Even if there is clear evidence that the strategies touted by The Know-It-All are out-of-date or proven by data to be ineffective, s/he cannot and will not be told otherwise. Blinders of so-called knowledge, blind spots, and obstacles are not perceived. And by "knowing without a doubt" one solution is the *right* solution, The Know-It-All can take a company into dangerous territory very quickly.

There are a few key phrases The Know-It-All will say, and they all involve an all-or-nothing principle:

- In my [vast number] years of experience, that has never/always worked.

- I have been doing this for a long time, and I can tell you without a doubt what works/doesn't work.

- I have been doing this so long, I can guarantee this will/won't work.

The Sleight-Of-Hand

The Sleight-of-Hand is by far the hardest to spot, and is my personal favorite. The Sleight-of-Hand is a master at masking his or her ineptitude long enough to wreak unmentionable havoc on a company's digital engagement strategy, and then is off to pollute another company.

The Sleight-of-Hand uses data to create the illusion great things are happening, with the exception of gaining market share and increasing sales. By cutting data or omitting certain aspects of the data picture, The Sleight-of-Hand can show incredible strides—almost too good to be true.

Because The Sleight-of-Hand is showing such amazing progress, no one in the organization wants to dig deeper and see if the results are true. That is where The Sleight-of-Hand gains his or her power, and where this type of consultant is the most dangerous. By selecting data points and changing the context, The Sleight-of-Hand can weave a realistic and believable story for executives.

Staff who want to probe deeper are rarely stopped by The Sleight-of-Hand. Instead, senior executives come to the defense of The Sleight-of-Hand. This is understandable, because The Sleight-of-Hand is making those executives look amazingly productive, even if that picture of productivity is short lived.

These are a few tricks The Sleight-of-Hand will deploy:

- Data points that are presented to show progress are usually the largest ones, such as millions of impressions on a digital ad. Large numbers are assumed to be positive.

- Data points are not explained as they relate to one another, or at all. The less the audience knows about the context around the data points, the better the picture The Sleight-of-Hand can imply.

- Application of data is rarely spoken of, since the data shows the current strategy is going so well, there is no need to change anything.

The One-Hit Wonder

The One-Hit Wonder thinks Plan A can work each and every time, and will apply Plan A even though that plan may have worked once, but is off the mark now. The One-Hit Wonder has a large hammer, and everything is treated like a nail.

While Plan A may work in some situations, Plan A is continuously applied even when mounting evidence indicates another strategy is required. There is a formula The One-Hit Wonder likes to use, and the execution of this formula is what is most important, not the final outcome.

The One-Hit Wonder may feel no need to mess with a prior success. Or The One-Hit Wonder may think that if this strategy is applied enough times, a successful engagement will be inevitable. Like *The Brady Bunch Movie*, The One-Hit Wonder will show the same architectural house, just with a different sign on it.

The issue with allowing the actions of The One-Hit Wonder can become an exponential problem: As the same ineffective engagement strategy is repeatedly deployed, the more distant customers and prospects become. Instead of continuing to climb, the company will actually be losing ground with digital engagement.

Want to catch The One-Hit Wonder in the act? Look out for these comments:

1. Just give this strategy a bit more time.

2. At [prior company], we always made this strategy work.

3. I am sure if we try this strategy again, we will see results.

The Guy/Gal On Your Side

The Guy/Gal On Your Side is the individual hired to say "Amen to that, John!" By always saying *yes*, this person ensures enough votes to push a strategy forward, whether or not the strategy makes any sense.

With The Guy/Gal On Your Side, typically a higher-level hire or consultant brought in to back up the thought process of a top executive, there is no strategic direction or leadership. The whole basis of bringing in The Guy/Gal On Your Side is to agree with whatever plan is developed.

What is most frightening about The Guy/Gal On Your Side is the freedom and power such a hire gives a top executive to develop a digital strategy that is not based on digital anything. By presenting a united front, business decisions not based on business considerations can be more easily approved and executed. Because of this ease of unilateral executive decisions backed by a so-called expert's sign-off, The Guy/Gal On Your Side is the most popular choice for corporations. This hire is almost like Christmas in July—irresistible, yet probably not the most reasonable scenario.

Tipoff phrases frequently used by The Guy/Gal On Your Side include:

1. I couldn't agree more.

2. Absolutely!

3. Without a doubt!

4. I have to side with [developer of the questionable strategy] on this one.

The Monsters We Have Created

Many companies will argue that these stereotypes have developed despite their efforts to bring on strong strategic partners and staff members. I argue that we have created these groups. They have come in because we have invited them to do so.

If a consultant interviewed at an organization and said that she or he was a strong digital marketer and still had 100 percent to learn, would that resonate or turn off the organization? If there was no opening for a "Yes man" or "Yes woman," would there be the phrase "Yes man" or "Yes woman?"

With all the effort and resources put into digital engagement, allowing just anyone into a company to determine strategic direction is akin to picking any surgeon at a hospital to operate on your only child. For someone who has founded her own company, my agency is like my child. I created my company from nothing. One moment there was no company; the next moment, there was.

The size or longevity of the organization is no match for any one of these four groups of hires. I have seen companies taken down in months by the wrong set of eyes on the road and hands on the wheel. Strategy is only as effective as the people executing the strategy. And strategic direction comes from understanding communication and how to engage in an authentic and meaningful way. Digital engagement has human hands all over the digital footprint.

Keeping all these things in focus in your digital house takes practice and patience. The culmination of these small activities and thoughtful developments can bring about huge digital dividends. Like anything, the mindful practice of fortifying your digital house will prepare you for whatever may come.

Guarding The Digital Fortress

Finding a strong player to add to your digital team does not have to feel like a search for a needle in a haystack. Key characteristics can define and identify this person.

1. Integrity. An individual with high integrity will work to complete something as best as she or he can and will let a company know if something is going wrong. When this person gives his or her word, a company can count on that.

2. Humility. This person will have a humble understanding of how complex and rapidly changing the digital world is and be open to adding to his or her arsenal of knowledge.

3. Desire for growth. Speaking of knowledge, wanting to constantly and continuously learn is a core value of the right individual, who will have a large base of working knowledge and will seek out ways to increase that knowledge. Knowledge gains are gains for the organization.

4. Confidence. This is not confidence
    in the traditional sense of the word.
    This is confidence to stand up and say
    something if the individual does not agree
    or has a different idea regarding how the
    strategy could go. In such a case, she or
    he will stand for the right path as if his or
    her life, and the organization's success,
    depended on that path.

5. Ownership. Even though the organization
    is not his or hers, this person will take
    responsibility and ownership as if it were.
    Having a personal investment in the
    success of the organization means every
    decision will be based on stewardship of
    the company, not on personal gain.

Chapter 8

Where We Go From Here

My goal in writing this book was to provide food for thought. When undergoing a digital transformation, a steady and methodical approach will beat a frenzied one any day. Business decisions not made with the business in mind can be catastrophic.

I had the opportunity to hear former Vice President Al Gore speak several years ago, and one sentence he stated rings true with me even to this day: "Extremes beget extremes." This philosophy can apply to digital decisions, where a big shift in digital strategy can cause a big turn-off for would-be readers.

Decisions made in panic mode tend to go in a direction that was not intended in the first place and create even bigger messes. Making smaller, incremental changes to your digital strategy allows a considered, careful approach that builds on itself. Broad-stroke changes done on a whim may or may not work and worse, can erode digital leverage instead of creating leverage.

In a similar way, not making digital engagement a true priority can slowly erode confidence in a company's digital message and connection with the audience. By the time a digital strategy is reviewed, the digital message may have floated away from any solid engagement, like an untied boat in the ocean.

Economic Uncertainty Can Come Out Of Left Field

The current American economic climate is in a state of uncertainty. Government operations were shut down in early 2019 for more than a full month, a historic moment that affected hundreds of thousands of government workers. What was most striking during that time was the number of interviews in which those middle-class workers shared, having already survived an economic recession only ten years ago, that they were still living paycheck-to-paycheck. Economic uncertainty is frequently unexpected and catches many off-guard.

A personal household is much more adept than an organization at managing change and can cut expenses and hunker down far faster than a company can. Constant vigilance around digital communication and messaging can provide one way to monitor the health of your message, the industry, and the customer base. With so much data available, companies have access to a wealth of tools, many of which were not available even twenty years ago, with which to find new prospects, gain international market share, and find and convert new customers.

By adjusting to emerging conditions and constantly reviewing data feedback, digital engagement can evolve and grow with the climate and status of prospects and customers so the organization's message is on point and applicable.

The Digital Triangle Perfected: Side One

Technology Review   Digital Message

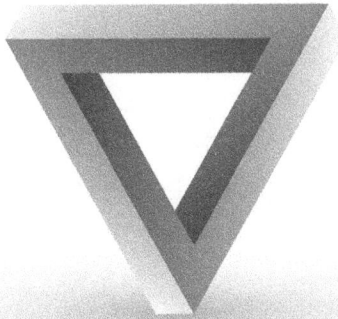

Data Application

In previous chapters, the means through which companies can fortify their digital strategy was explored, covering three main elements. Each element can be thought of as a side of a triangle. The three sides to the digital triangle provide the focus and balance to perfect and maintain digital engagement: data application, technology review and digital messaging.

Data application is the first side of the triangle. The focus should be on choosing and capturing appropriate data points. For example, if a company has posted a new video to show a new product, appropriate data points to measure engagement would include click rate, how long the video was viewed, and if the call to action was followed (in this instance, visiting the website for more information). When companies start to take responsibility for how data is captured and which data points are chosen, they begin to see patterns and trends in their data. This leads to appropriate data application. In the above example, if data tracking shows the viewers abandon watching the video at the 30 second mark and the video is a minute long, the organization could try to reduce the video to 30 seconds to see if the video is watched to the end.

Many companies take a backseat when it comes to collecting, analyzing, understanding, and applying their data. No one should know and understand your data better than you. Data keeps tabs on the health and trajectory of an organization and should be monitored closely.

Side Two Of The Digital Triangle

Technology review helps companies understand how customers and prospects find and engage with digital content. This is the second side of the digital triangle. The mode in which customers consume content is as important as the content itself. Each new technology advancement changes the behavior of how users engage with digital content. Think of how someone would eat if he or she had a spoon versus a fork, or chopsticks instead of silverware. Foods would be prepared differently; cut to different sizes or include broth (or not), for example. Rice in a dish that uses chopsticks tends to be sticky rice.

By actively engaging and using technology in everyday life, companies can get a hint of how customers and prospects will use the same technology to engage with their brand message. Observe the world, your family and friends, and colleagues and evaluate what technology is in their arsenal.

Digital Triangle Completed: Side Three

The last side of the digital triangle is the digital message. The digital message is a living, breathing organism that grows and expands, morphs and modifies, as the climate and needs of the prospect changes. Or at least the digital message *should* change.

Companies sometimes forget the life that is inside their digital message. Like living energy, the digital message needs to be allowed room to grow and change. Instead, companies keep the digital message exactly the same, season after season, year after year.

They say in combat that if you are not advancing, you are retreating. Even holding ground requires a forward effort. Why would an organization's digital engagement not also need to keep moving forward? Keeping digital messaging that is stale creates engagement that can become stale.

Digital messaging does not need radical change, but it does need room for growth and modification. Small tweaks keep the brand fresh while still maintaining the core values of the brand. The personality of the brand should always be kept intact, and making minor shifts in brand story keeps the core value of the brand in sight.

Bringing These Three Sides Together

These three sides of the triangle come together in a way that builds on each part and becomes more than the sum. Data capture and application only work when the technology is deployed with the digital message intact. Technology deployment provides the means to capture the data, which is done through the digital message.

In the center of this triangle are both the provider of digital engagement (the organization) and the consumers of digital content (the prospect and customer). And while a triangle has clear points where sides start and end, the digital triangle constantly ebbs and flows, moving in and out and around the human element in a whirlwind fashion. With so many ways each side can and will change, there is no pause in the triangle's energy and movement, almost like a beating pulse bringing lifeblood to those working and interacting with digital content.

I have seen companies who look at digital engagement as static and miss the energy and flow within the digital world. Like weather patterns, while there is some predictability, there is also chaos and power that can quickly overtake and humble even the best of us. But with steady review and commitment to an organization's digital world, so much learning can be created, taking that organization to a new level of digital purpose.

Guarding The Digital Fortress

Before we part, let me leave with a final request. I am asking companies to do something that may feel foreign: Be proactive in an organization's digital health.

1. **Tweak along the way.** Instead of waiting until something bad is happening to start to put a company's digital house in order, tweak things along the way. Be calm and resilient under pressure, and create a business and digital message that are thriving long before any economic downturn hits.

2. **Play the long game.** These strategies and methodologies can be added to an organization's weekly business review without much modification to schedule. The consideration that may need to be overcome is that digital engagement is a long game. There are some short wins, but those who do well stick with their digital strategy review and continue to move that strategy forward. Even when a miscalculation or stumble happens, the company knows that the time and effort put into working its digital communication will pay off and get it through current challenges.

3. **No silver bullet exists to slay the digital beast.** Digital strategy and a

strong digital brand take time to build, cultivate and share. Likewise, each company is unique in how customers and prospects engage with and understand the brand. Finding an organization's nuances and translating those nuances to digital form take work and dedication, but the end result is more than worth the effort.

4. **Prioritization is the priority.**
Prioritization of digital strategy provides information, so when there is a digital storm, that storm is much easier to weather. Give your company that prioritization and keep the digital conversation going with authentic engagement. When the next digital storm approaches, your organization can be prepared. The competition may not be, which will clear a path for new market growth and new customers. When the dust settles and companies and customers emerge on the other side, your digital voice will have been the constant.

About The Author

L isa Apolinski is an international speaker, author, and digital strategist. She is considered a digital engagement thought leader and has worked in the industry for more than two decades. Her focus is on the end-user experience, whether the venue, technology, or communication.

She is the founder and CEO of 3 Dog Write Inc., a full-service digital consulting agency. 3 Dog Write provides strategic consulting around digital engagement and creation and proper use of digital assets.

Lisa serves on the board at the University of South Florida for the digital marketing program certificate. She has guest lectured at Columbia University and has been featured in *Forbes* multiple times, sharing her insight and expertise on digital marketing growth strategies.

Lisa lives in the Phoenix area with her family and rescue dogs. She is always up for a cup of coffee and a conversation on digital strategy. She can be reached at lisa@3dogwrite.com.

Acknowledgments

While I have so many people I could thank, three people stand out on my list. First and foremost, I wish to thank my editor and mentor, Henry DeVries. His encouragement was the reason I chose to write a book and why I have a finished book.

Second, I wish to thank my good friend Diana Nemes. She attended a lecture by an amazing consultant and thought to purchase one of the available books for me. That book shifted my business focus and moved my agency to the next level.

And finally, I would not have the career and life I have without the advice from my sister Valerie. For that, I will be eternally grateful and cannot thank her enough.

Works Cited

"37 Mind Blowing YouTube Facts, Figures and Statistics –
2019." MerchDope. February 19, 2019. Accessed
February 27, 2019. https://merchdope.com/
youtube-stats/.

"Are Declining Attention Spans Killing Your Content
Marketing Strategy?" Cision.com January 22,
2018. Accessed February 27, 2019. https://www.
cision.com/us/2018/01/declining-attention-killing-
content-marketing-strategy/.

Chaffey, Dave. "Global Social Media Research Summary
2019." Smart Insights. February 12, 2019.
Accessed February 27, 2019. https://www.
smartinsights.com/social-media-marketing/social-
media-strategy/new-global-social-media-research/.

Cooper, Paige. "22 YouTube Stats That Matter to
Marketers in 2019." Hootsuite Social Media
Management. January 23, 2019. Accessed April
14, 2019. https://blog.hootsuite.com/youtube-
stats-marketers/.

Cooper, Paige. "Social Media Advertising Stats That
Matter to Marketers in 2018." Hootsuite Social
Media Management. June 06, 2018. Accessed
February 26, 2019. https://blog.hootsuite.com/
social-media-advertising-stats/.

Durden, Tyler. "Do economic or industry factors affect
business survival?" Small Business Administration
Office of Advocacy Small Business Facts, June
2012. Accessed February 26, 2019. https://www.
sba.gov/sites/default/files/Business-Survival.pdf.

"Everything Is Fake": Ex-Reddit CEO Confirms Internet
Traffic Metrics Are Bullshit." Zero Hedge.
December 27, 2018. Accessed February 26,
2019. https://www.zerohedge.com/news/2018-
12-27/everything-fake-ex-reddit-ceo-confirms-
internet-traffic-metrics-are-bullshit.

"Facebook Is Sued for 'inflating' Ad Watch times by up
to 900% to Lure in Advertisers." RT International.
October 17, 2018. Accessed February 26, 2019.
https://www.rt.com/usa/441569-facebook-
inflated-video-numbers.

Hollander, Rayna. "Two-thirds of the World's Population
Are Now Connected by Mobile Devices."
Business Insider. September 19, 2017. Accessed
February 27, 2019. https://www.businessinsider.
com/world-population-mobile-devices-2017-9.

Leighton, Mara. "6 New Lingerie Companies That Are Changing the Industry - with Inclusive Sizes and a Woman-led Design Process." Business Insider. July 08, 2018. Accessed February 21, 2019. https://www.businessinsider.com/new-lingerie-brands-2018-6.

Loechner, Jack. "Brand Loyalty Not A Millennial Trait." Mediapost.com. March 30, 2018. Accessed February 27, 2019. https://www.mediapost.com/publications/article/316190/brand-loyalty-not-a-millennial-trait.html.

Miners, Zach. "The Average Mobile YouTube Session Is Now 40 Minutes, Google Says." CIO. July 16, 2015. Accessed April 14, 2019. http://www.cio.com/article/2949473/the-average-mobile-youtube-session-is-now-40-minutes-google-says.html.

"New Survey from Curalate Finds 76% of Consumers Purchase Products They Discover on Social Media, across All Social Channels." *Business Wire*. November 15, 2017. Accessed February 26, 2019. https://www.businesswire.com/news/home/20171115006040/en/New-Survey-Curalate-Finds-76-Consumers-Purchase.

"Content Shock: Why Content Marketing Is Not a Sustainable Strategy." Schaefer Marketing Solutions: We Help Businesses {grow}. November 29, 2017. Accessed April 14, 2019. https:// businessesgrow.com/2014/01/06/content-shock/.

Smith, Kit. "122 Amazing Social Media Statistics and Facts." Brandwatch. March 1, 2019. Accessed February 27, 2019. https://www.brandwatch. com/blog/amazing-social-media-statistics-and-facts/.

"Tech Is at the Heart of ThirdLove's Success, Co-CEO Heidi Zak Says." Bloomberg.com. October 05, 2018. Accessed February 21, 2019. https://www. bloomberg.com/news/videos/2018-10-05/tech-is-at-the-heart-of-thirdlove-s-success-co-ceo-heidi-zak-says-video.

"Time Flies: U.S. Adults Now Spend Nearly Half a Day Interacting with Media." What People Watch, Listen To and Buy. Accessed February 27, 2019. https://www.nielsen.com/us/en/insights/news/2018/time-flies-us-adults-now-spend-nearly-half-a-day-interacting-with-media.print.html.